Music Notation Primer

Glen R. Rosencrans

Amsco Publications
New York/London/Sydney

Order No. AM 26642
International Standard Book Number: 0.8256.9149.4
Library of Congress Catalog Card Number: 79-87711

Exclusive Distributors:
Music Sales Corporation
225 Park Avenue South, New York, NY 10003, USA
Music Sales Limited
8/9 Frith Street, London W1V 5TZ England
Music Sales Pty. Limited
120 Rothschild Street, Rosebery, Sydney, NSW 2018, Australia

Printed in the United States of America by
Vicks Lithograph and Printing Corporation

To Ernie....

Special thanx to

LILE CRUSE FOR A CREATIVE SPACE TO STRETCH OUT IN, TO ERNIE ROSECRANS AND HIS NEVER ENDING COUNSEL, TO PETER PICKOW FOR SUCH PRECISE EDITING, AND TO SO MANY PEOPLE WHOSE HELP HAS BEEN IMMEASURABLE: PATTI FOX, JIM McFARLIN, ERIC SPRITZER, RUTH CHRISTENSON, OLAF SCHIAPPACASSE, JOHN LIVINGSTON, LORRAINE ROSECRANS, PATRICIA OBREGON AND TO MY STUDENTS FOR THEIR NEVER ENDING QUESTIONS.

CONTENTS

PREFACE ~

THIS IS A LITTLE BOOK FOR THOSE WHO WISH TO BE-
COME NEATER IN THEIR MUSICAL NOTATION. AFTER
TEACHING AND LECTURING IN COLLEGES FOR A FEW
YEARS NOW, I HAVE SEEN A GREAT NEED FOR STUDENTS
TO BECOME MORE LEGIBLE IN THEIR WRITING. THIS
BOOK THEN, IS BORN OUT OF THIS VISION.

IN A SENSE THIS IS A CALLIGRAPHY STUDY. IN OTHER
WORDS, HOW TO WRITE MUSIC WITH PEN AND INK. IT IS
AN ESSENTIAL STUDY FOR ORCHESTRATION STUDENTS
WHO NEED TO HAVE THEIR PARTS PLAYED AND FOR
THEORY STUDENTS WHO WISH TO PRESENT THEIR LARG-
ER PROJECTS IN FINISHED FORM. OF COURSE, BY
STUDYING PEN AND INK WRITING, ORDINARY PENCIL
WRITING IMPROVES AS WELL.

IT HAS OFTEN BEEN SAID THAT IT IS MORE DIFFICULT
TO DECIDE WHAT TO LEAVE OUT OF A BOOK THAN WHAT
TO PUT IN IT. THIS HAS CERTAINLY BEEN THE CASE HERE.
I HAVE TRIED TO MAKE A NORMALLY DRY SUBJECT AS
LIGHT AS POSSIBLE, BOILING ALL THE MATERIAL ON NO-
TATION DOWN TO ITS ESSENCE. IN DOING SO IT WAS
NECESSARY TO LEAVE MUCH OUT. BUT WHAT I HAVE
AIMED AT IS COMMON WRITING SITUATIONS, NOT
SPECIALTY PROBLEMS. I HOPE I HAVE BEEN SUC-
CESSFUL IN MY EFFORTS.

MAKE GOOD FRIENDS WITH THIS BOOK. USE IT FOR
REFERENCE WHENEVER YOU WRITE. READ THE LAST
PAGES ON LAYOUTS FIRST, BROWSE THRU THE MID-
DLE, THEN START FROM THE FRONT.

G.R.

Tools and Materials

PELIKAN 120 PEN WITH OBLIQUE MEDIUM TIP FOR DRAWING MUSIC SYMBOLS.
or
OSMIROID FOUNTAIN PEN WITH MUSIC WRITING POINT.

TRY THE FELT TIP PASSANTINO MUSIC PEN FOR MORE CASUAL WRITING.

FINE OR MEDIUM TIP FOUNTAIN PEN FOR LETTERING AND DRAWING EXTRA SMALL THINGS.

SPEEDBALL PEN WITH B-1 OR B-2 NIB FOR TITLEING.

6"
3½"
SMALL TRANSPARENT PLASTIC TRIANGLE

9½"
4"
SMALL HAND BLOTTER

PAPER:
8/10 STAVE WIDE LINE WITH TITLE SPACE. USE HEAVY, (36 LB) HIGHLY POLISHED PAPER.

HIGGINS BLACK INDIA INK

INK

TRANSPARENT TAPE TO TAPE PAGES TOGETHER

RUBBER CEMENT

INK ERASER

SINGLE EDGE RAZOR BLADE OR SCISSORS TO CUT STRIPS OF STAFF PAPER TO GLUE OVER MISTAKES.

FINE 600-A SANDPAPER TO SMOOTH EDGE OF A ROUGH PEN

SMALL COTTON RAG FOR WIPING PEN CLEAN

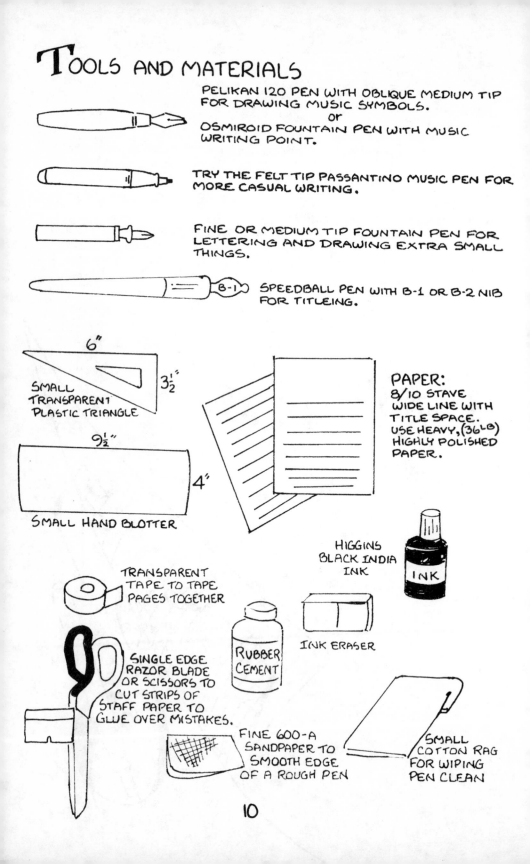

KEEP YOUR MATERIALS IN AN ARTIST'S POUCH OR CARRYING CASE. IT'S IMPORTANT TO USE HIGH QUALITY PAPER. THIN WEIGHT PAPER WON'T HOLD THE INK AND YOUR WORK WILL SUFFER FOR IT.

ALWAYS KEEP YOUR PENS CLEAN. IF YOU'RE NOT GOING TO USE THEM FOR A COUPLE OF DAYS WASH THEM OUT WITH WATER TO KEEP THE INK FROM DRYING AND CLOGGING. A CLOGGED PEN CAN BE FREED WITH AMMONIA OR PEN CLEANER.

GOOD WORK HABITS ARE INSEPERABLE FROM GOOD WORK. RESPECT YOUR MATERIALS AND THEY WILL WORK WELL FOR YOU. ALWAYS WORK ON A LARGE FLAT SURFACE. GIVE YOURSELF PLENTY OF ROOM AND GOOD LIGHTING.

DON'T FORCE YOUR PEN INTO THE PAPER. YOU'LL GET OPTIMUM PREFORMANCE FROM IT WRITING LIGHTLY. IT'S A DELICATE INSTRUMENT THAT SHOULD GLIDE ACROSS THE PAPER.

WRITE TO ANY OF THESE 'MUSIC WRITERS SUPPLY' STORES AND THEY WILL BE HAPPY TO SEND YOU FREE CATALOGUES WITH MANY FINE PAPERS AND MATERIALS LISTED IN THEM:

- PASSANTINO MUSIC WRITING SUPPLIES - 33 WEST 60TH ST. NEW YORK, N.Y. 10023
- ALPHEUS MUSIC CORP. ~ 1433 N. COLE PL., HOLLYWOOD, CA.
- ROGER FERRIS MUSIC - 1527½ N. VINE ST., HOLLYWOOD, CA.
- VALLE MUSIC - 12441 RIVERSIDE DR., N. HOLLYWOOD, CA.
- KING BRAND MUSIC - 1595 BROADWAY, NEW YORK, N.Y.

First Strokes

MAKE SURE THE POINT ON YOUR PEN IS SCREWED IN TIGHTLY. FILL THE PEN AND TRY IT ON A PIECE OF PRACTICE PAPER. IF IT DOESN'T WRITE 'THROW' THE INK DOWN THRU THE CHANNEL BY SHAKING IT IN A SHARP DOWNWARD MOTION ABOVE YOUR BLOTTER. THE INK SHOULD SPLASH OUT. WIPE THE NIB CLEAN AND START TO WRITE.

THE PEN IS CUT AT A 30° ANGLE AND MUST BE FLUSH WITH THE PAPER TO WRITE. THIS WILL PUT THE ANGLE AT WHICH YOU HOLD YOUR PEN AT ABOUT 60°. THIS WILL BE YOUR NORMAL WRITING POSITION.

ANGLE MUST BE FLUSH WITH PAPER TO WRITE

NEVER 'TWRIL' THE PEN INTO DIF-FERENT POSITIONS. ITS UNNECES-SARY AND WILL ONLY SLOW YOU DOWN.

EAST TO WEST LINES ARE HEAVY (BEAMS, WHOLE RESTS, ETC.)

NORTH TO SOUTH LINES ARE THIN AND ARE ALWAYS DRAWN EXACTLY PERPENDICULAR TO THE BOTTOM OF THE PAGE. (BAR LINES, STEMS, ETC.)

WHEN CURVED LINES ARE DRAWN, THE WIDTH OF THE LINE CHANGES WITH THE CURVE, CREATING A SLIGHT SHADING EF-FECT. THIS COMES AS A RESULT OF HOLDING THE PEN IN ITS CONSTANT ANGLE THROUGHOUT THE CURVE. (TREBLE CLEFS, BASS CLEFS, FLAGS, ETC.)

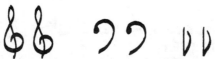

NOTE:
REFRENCES ARE MADE THROUGHOUT THE BOOK TO YOUR 'SMALL PEN'. THIS MEANS USE YOUR FINE OR MEDIUM POINT FOUNTAIN PEN. YOUR 'REGULAR PEN' MEANS YOUR CHISEL EDGE OSMIROID OR PELIKAN PEN.

THE TRIANGLE IS HELD IN YOUR LEFT HAND WHILE YOU WORK. THE PEN RUNS ALONG THE TRIANGLE ACTING AS A STRAIGHT EDGE.

GUIDE FOR E.W. LINES

GUIDE FOR N.S. LINES

THIS EDGE RESTS ON THE PAPER

THESE FINGERS WILL PROP THE TRIANGLE ABOUT 3/8" FROM THE PAPER, KEEPING IT FROM COMING IN CONTACT WITH THE WET INK.

THIS EDGE RESTS ON THE PAPER

TOP OF TRIANGLE. GUIDE FOR EAST-WEST LINES. (BEAM LINES)

THIS EDGE IS THE ONLY ONE RESTING FLAT ON THE PAPER.

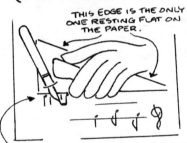

THE PEN IS ACTUALLY RUNNING ALONG EDGE OF TRIANGLE JUST SLIGHTLY ELEVATED BY FINGERTIPS.

SIDE OF TRIANGLE. GUIDE FOR NORTH-SOUTH LINES. (STEM AND BAR LINES)

THIS EDGE IS THE ONLY ONE RESTING FLAT ON THE PAPER.

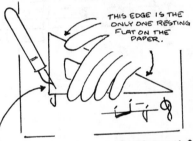

TIP OF PEN ANGLES UNDER TRIANGLE WHEN USING IT ALONG THIS SIDE EDGE.

THROUGHOUT THE BOOK YOU WILL SEE SMALL PICTURES OF TRIANGLES SUGGESTING WHICH SIDE TO USE ON EACH OF THE SYMBOLS.

USE THIS SIDE OF THE TRIANGLE

USE THIS SIDE OF THE TRIANGLE

TURN THE TRIANGLE SIDEWAYS & USE THIS SIDE.

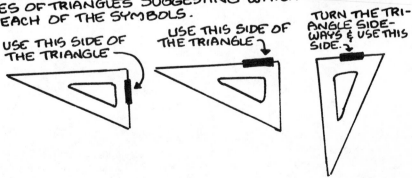

WHEN INK COLLECTS ALONG THE EDGES OF YOUR
TRIANGLE, WIPE IT OFF ON YOUR BLOTTER. THIS
IS A CONSTANT PROCESS. IF YOU
DON'T CHECK THE EDGES CONSTANT-
LY YOU'LL FIND INK DRIPPING OFF
ONTO YOUR WORK.

Mistakes!

IF YOU CAN'T ERASE A MISTAKE WITH YOUR INK
ERASER, CUT OUT A PIECE OF STAFF LINE FROM AN
EXTRA PAGE AND GLUE IT OVER THE MISTAKE.

IF YOU PHOTO COPY THE
PAGE THE PATCH WON'T SHOW.

CLEFS

TREBLE CLEF

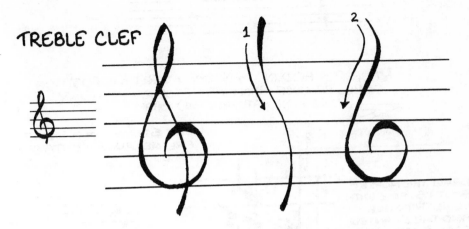

BASS CLEF

ALTO CLEF, TENOR CLEF

SHARPS, FLATS, AND ACCIDENTALS

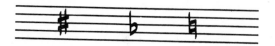

YOUR PEN HELD IN ITS NORMAL WRITING POSITION WILL PRODUCE THIN LINES CROSSED BY HEAVY ONES ON NATURALS AND SHARPS.

THE STEMS ON A SHARP ARE NEARLY AN OCTAVE TALL.

DRAW THE NORTH-SOUTH STEMS WITH YOUR TRIANGLE AND THE SLANTED EAST-WEST LINES FREEHAND.

"OFF SET" PARALLEL STEMS

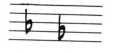

WHEN A FLAT IS IN A SPACE, THE STEM EXTENDS TO THE SECOND SPACE ABOVE IT. IF IT'S ON A LINE IT EXTENDS TO THE SECOND LINE ABOVE IT.

USE THE TRIANGLE ON THE STEM, THEN ATTACH A FREEHAND HALF HEART TO IT.

IF A NATURAL IS ON A LINE, IT'S STEMS GO TO THE NEAR-EST SPACE IN EITHER DIREC-TION. IF ITS IN A SPACE, THEY EXTEND TO THE NEAREST LINES.

DRAW THE NORTH-SOUTH STEMS WITH YOUR TRIANGLE AND THE SLANTED EAST-WEST LINES FREEHAND.

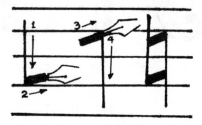

16

KEY SIGNATURES

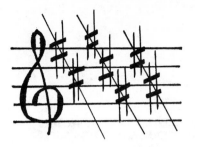 

NOTICE THE SYMMETRICAL LAYOUT

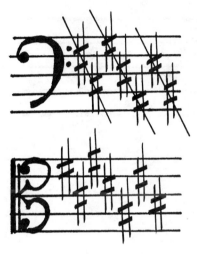 

DOUBLE SHARPS, DOUBLE FLATS

DOUBLE SHARP

DRAW AN 'X' WITH YOUR PEN HELD IN ITS NORMAL
WRITING POSITION. YOU WILL PRODUCE A THIN LINE
CROSSED BY A FAT ONE.

THEN ADD THE DOTS

DOUBLE FLAT

TWO NORMAL FLATS DRAWN VERY CLOSE TO EACH OTHER.

TIME SIGNATURES

USE LARGE BOLD NUMBERS:

TOP NUMBER
SITS ON THIRD
LINE

BOTTOM NUMBER
EXTENDS UP TO
THIRD LINE

THE NUMBERS
STRETCH ABOUT 1/8"
OVER EACH SIDE OF THE
STAFF.

AN EASY WAY
TO DRAW 4

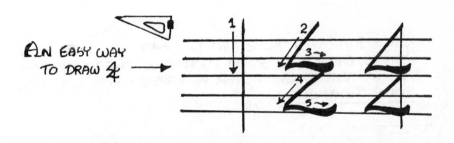

COMMON TIME

ADD
SHADING

ALLA BREVE

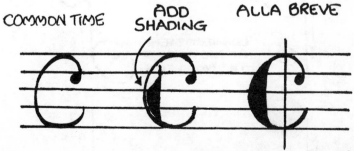

ADD HOOK AND DRAW A
STRAIGHT LINE WITH YOUR TRI-
ANGLE FOR ALLA BREVE (2/2).

WHOLE, HALF, AND QUARTER NOTES

NOTEHEADS ARE OVAL.

DRAW THE OPEN NOTEHEAD
WITH ONE CONTINUOUS STROKE.

NOTE THE AXIS
OF THE OVAL

A SOLID NOTEHEAD IS
DRAWN WITH A SPIRAL
MOVEMENT, STARTING
FROM THE INSIDE OUT.

NOTE THE AXIS
OF THE OVAL

STEMS ARE ATTACHED TO THE OVAL AT THE AXIS
POINTS. DRAW THE STEM TO THE NOTEHEAD OR FROM
THE NOTEHEAD, WHICHEVER IS EASIER FOR YOU. USE
YOUR TRIANGLE.

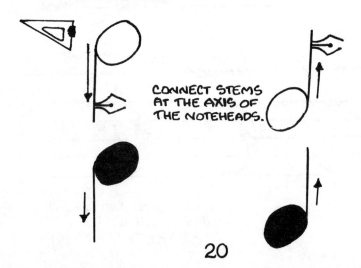

CONNECT STEMS
AT THE AXIS OF
THE NOTEHEADS.

STEMS ARE ABOUT
AN OCTAVE LONG.

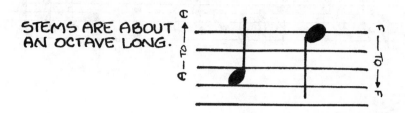

ANY NOTE FROM THE 3RD LINE
UP WILL HAVE A "DOWN" STEM.

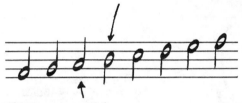

ANY NOTE FROM THE 2ND SPACE
DOWN WILL HAVE AN "UP" STEM.

"AIR SPACE"

WHEN YOU'RE DRAWING NOTES
ON EITHER SIDE OF THE STAFF,
LEAVE A LITTLE AIR SPACE BE-
TWEEN THE NOTE AND THE STAFF;
THIS KEEPS THE NOTE CLEARLY
DEFINED.

THE NOTE-AND-STEM STROKE COMBINATION ARE THE
MOST FREQUENT PEN MOVEMENTS USED IN MUSIC
CALLIGRAPHY. THERE IS OFTEN A TENDENCY FOR THE
WRITER TO DRAW THE NOTEHEAD WITH HIS HAND IN
ONE POSITION AND THEN RELOCATE HIS HAND IN ANOTH-
ER POSITION TO DRAW THE STEM. THIS "RELOCATING"
THE HAND CAN GET TO BE QUITE LONG-WINDED AND
CLUMSY. IF YOU EXPERIMENT YOU WILL FIND ONE HAND
POSITION FROM WHICH YOU WILL BE ABLE TO DRAW
NOTE AND STEM CORRECTLY AND QUICKLY.

THE TRIANGLE TAKES SOME GETTING USED TO AL-
SO, BUT THE EXTRA EFFORT IS WORTH IT TO GET CLEAN,
STRAIGHT STEMS.

21

FLAGS

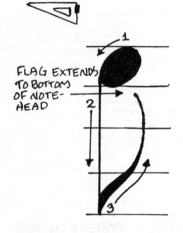

FLAG EXTENDS TO BOTTOM OF NOTE-HEAD

FLAG EXTENDS TO BOTTOM OF NOTEHEAD

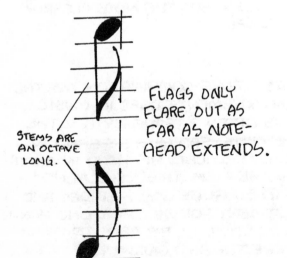

STEMS ARE AN OCTAVE LONG.

FLAGS ONLY FLARE OUT AS FAR AS NOTE-HEAD EXTENDS.

BE CAREFUL NOT TO LET FLAG FLARE OUT TOO MUCH.

16TH AND 32ND NOTES

16TH NOTE

STEM STILL AN OCTAVE LONG. DRAW INSIDE FLAG FIRST, STARTING TWO STAFF DEGREES BACK FROM THE END OF THE STEM.*

TWO STAFF DEGREES

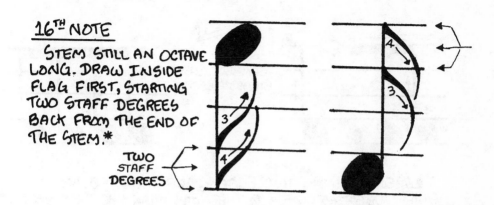

32ND NOTE

SAME AS THE 16TH NOTE BUT EXTEND STEM LENGTH TWO DEGREES AND ADD THE LAST FLAG THERE.

MAKE STEM TWO STAFF DEGREES LONGER

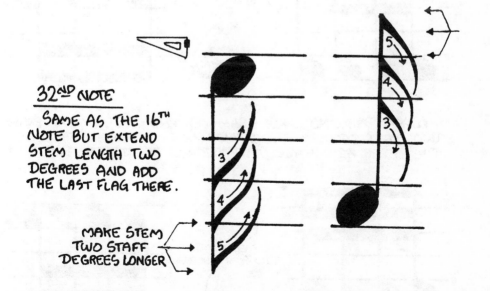

* A STAFF DEGREE IS THE DISTANCE FROM A LINE TO THE SPACE NEAREST IT AND VICE VERSA.

BEAMS

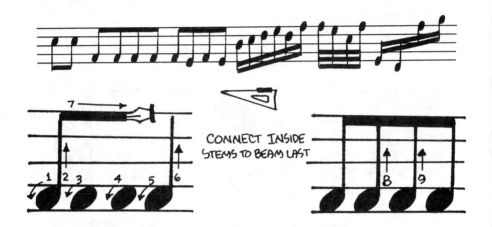

WHEN DRAWING TWO BEAMS, ADD THE 2ND BEAM TWO STAFF DEGREES CLOSER TO THE NOTES THAN THE FIRST BEAM.

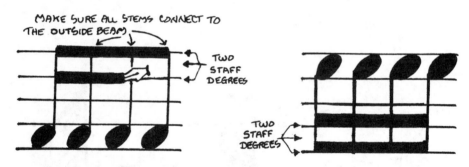

WHEN DRAWING THREE BEAMS, EXTEND THE STEMS AN EXTRA TWO STAFF DEGREES AND DRAW THE FIRST BEAM THERE. ADD THE OTHER BEAMS TWO STAFF DEGREES APART FROM EACH OTHER.

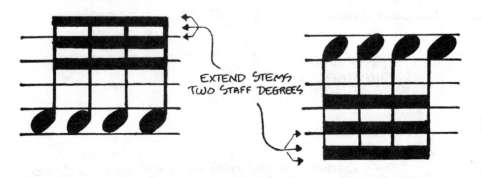

IF MOST OF THE STEMS IN THE GROUP OF NOTES GO UP, THEN THE BEAM GOES OVER THE NOTES, AND <u>ALL</u> OF THE STEMS IN THE GROUP WILL BE TURNED UP TO MEET THE BEAM, AND VICE VERSA.

THE CONTEXT OF THE PHRASE WILL DETERMINE WHICH SIDE THE BEAM SHOULD BE ON HERE.

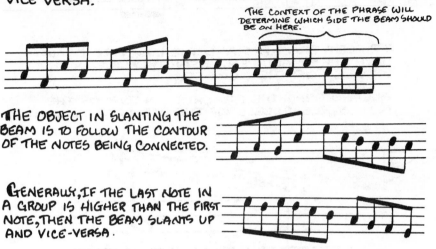

THE OBJECT IN SLANTING THE BEAM IS TO FOLLOW THE CONTOUR OF THE NOTES BEING CONNECTED.

GENERALLY, IF THE LAST NOTE IN A GROUP IS HIGHER THAN THE FIRST NOTE, THEN THE BEAM SLANTS UP AND VICE-VERSA.

IF THE FIRST AND LAST NOTES OF A GROUP ARE THE SAME, OR IF A BEAM CONNECTS TWO ALTERNATING NOTES, THEN THE BEAM WILL BE STRAIGHT.

LIKE THIS:

NOT THIS:

LIKE THIS:

NOT THIS:

SOMETIMES PLACING THE BEAM BETWEEN THE NOTES WILL BE MORE GRACEFUL NOTATION INSTEAD OF DRAWING EXCEEDINGLY LONG STEMS, ESPECIALLY IF THE SPACE BETWEEN THE STAVES IS CROWDED.

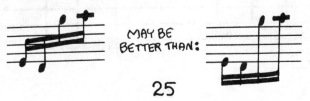

MAY BE BETTER THAN:

25

TRIPLET BRACKETS

TRIPLET BRACKETS AND THE LIKE ARE DRAWN
WITH THE SMALL PEN. BREAK THE LINE IN THE
MIDDLE FOR THE NUMBER.

ALWAYS DRAW THE BRACKET ON TOP OF THE
NOTES, REGARDLESS OF THE STEM DIRECTION.

LEGER LINES

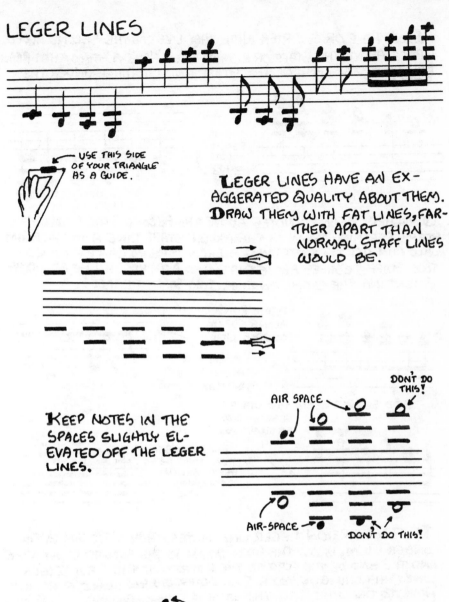

USE THIS SIDE OF YOUR TRIANGLE AS A GUIDE.

LEGER LINES HAVE AN EX-AGGERATED QUALITY ABOUT THEM. DRAW THEM WITH FAT LINES, FARTHER APART THAN NORMAL STAFF LINES WOULD BE.

KEEP NOTES IN THE SPACES SLIGHTLY ELEVATED OFF THE LEGER LINES.

AIR SPACE

DON'T DO THIS!

AIR-SPACE

DON'T DO THIS!

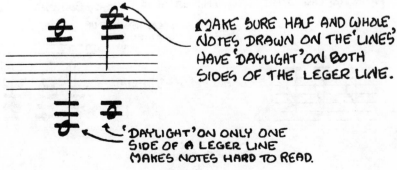

MAKE SURE HALF AND WHOLE NOTES DRAWN ON THE 'LINES' HAVE 'DAYLIGHT' ON BOTH SIDES OF THE LEGER LINE.

'DAYLIGHT' ON ONLY ONE SIDE OF A LEGER LINE MAKES NOTES HARD TO READ.

ANY HALF OR QUARTER NOTE THAT LIES ON THE SECOND ADDED SPACE ABOVE THE STAFF OR HIGHER WILL HAVE A STEM THAT REACHES THE MIDDLE LINE OF THE STAFF AND LIKEWISE UNDER THE STAFF.

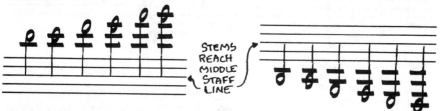

STEMS REACH MIDDLE STAFF LINE

SIMILARLY, BEAMED NOTES ABOVE THE SECOND SPACE WILL HAVE STEMS REACHING DOWN TO THE MIDDLE STAFF LINE AND THE BEAM WILL RUN ACROSS THAT LINE. A SECOND BEAM CAN BE ADDED TWO STAFF DEGREES ABOVE THAT, AND A THIRD CAN BE ADDED BY EXTENDING THE STEMS ANOTHER TWO STAFF DEGREES.

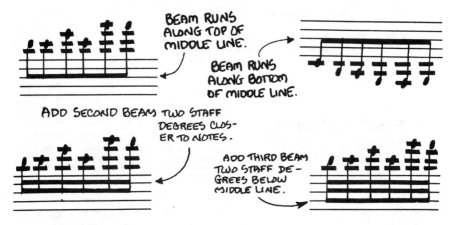

BEAM RUNS ALONG TOP OF MIDDLE LINE.

BEAM RUNS ALONG BOTTOM OF MIDDLE LINE.

ADD SECOND BEAM TWO STAFF DEGREES CLOSER TO NOTES.

ADD THIRD BEAM TWO STAFF DEGREES BELOW MIDDLE LINE.

IF FLAGS ARE ON LEGER LINE NOTES, THEY NEED AN EVEN LONGER STEM. DRAW THE STEM DOWN TO THE SECOND STAFF SPACE AND THE END OF THE FLAG TO THE BOTTOM OF THE FIRST LEDGER LINE. THIS WILL GIVE YOU A FULL OCTAVE, AS YOU WOULD NORMALLY HAVE, TO DRAW THE FLAG. THE SAME IS TRUE, OF COURSE, IN REVERSE.

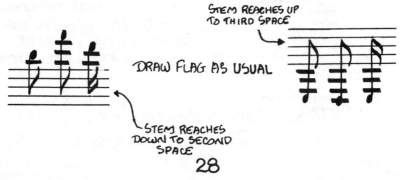

STEM REACHES UP TO THIRD SPACE

DRAW FLAG AS USUAL

STEM REACHES DOWN TO SECOND SPACE

DOTS

WHEN THE NOTE IS IN A SPACE, THE DOT GOES IN THE SPACE WITH IT.	WHEN THE NOTE IS ON A LINE, THE DOT GOES ON THE SPACE ABOVE.

THE SAME IS TRUE FOR LEGER LINE NOTES.

IF THE NOTE IS ON A LINE AND HAS A DOWN FLAG THE DOT IS PLACED ON THE SPACE ABOVE THE NOTE AND BEYOND THE FLAG.

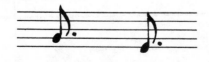

RESTS

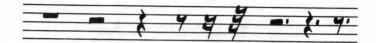

ALL RESTS ARE DRAWN FREEHAND

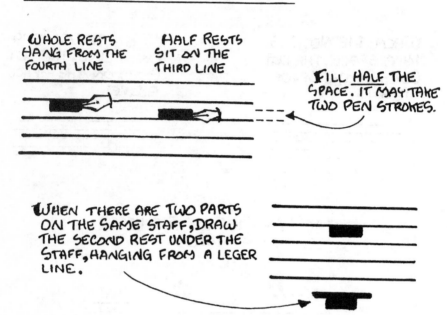

WHOLE RESTS HANG FROM THE FOURTH LINE

HALF RESTS SIT ON THE THIRD LINE

FILL HALF THE SPACE. IT MAY TAKE TWO PEN STROKES.

WHEN THERE ARE TWO PARTS ON THE SAME STAFF, DRAW THE SECOND REST UNDER THE STAFF, HANGING FROM A LEGER LINE.

QUARTER REST

THE 1/8 REST
SITS IN THE
SECOND AND
THIRD SPACES.

THE 16TH REST STEM
REACHES THE BOTTOM OF
THE STAFF. THE SECOND
HOOK IS IN THE SECOND
SPACE.

THE 32ND REST REACHES
TO THE TOP OF THE STAFF.
THE THIRD HOOK IS IN THE
TOP SPACE.

THE 64TH REST IS LIKE
THE 32ND WITH ONE MORE
HOOK IN THE BOTTOM
SPACE.

DOTTED RESTS

MOST DOTS ARE IN 3RD STAFF SPACE

DOTS PLACED
AFTER 32ND
AND 64TH RESTS
ARE IN THE
TOP SPACE.

MULTIPLE BAR RESTS

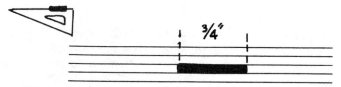

WITH A FEW PEN STROKES AND WITH THE TRIANGLE, DRAW A HEAVY LINE THAT FILLS UP THE SECOND SPACE ABOUT 3/4" LONG.

DRAW TWO NORTH-SOUTH LINES AT BOTH ENDS OF THE HEAVY LINE THAT REACH FROM THE BOTTOM LINE OF THE STAFF TO THE 4TH LINE.

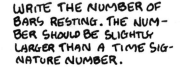

WRITE THE NUMBER OF BARS RESTING. THE NUMBER SHOULD BE SLIGHTLY LARGER THAN A TIME SIGNATURE NUMBER.

IN BRACED PARTS DRAW THE HEAVY LINES IN BOTH STAVES AND THE NUMBER IN BETWEEN THEM.

DYNAMIC MARKS

pp p mp mf f ff

FOR THE "PIANO" SIGN,
DRAW A SLANTED LINE AND
ADD A WHOLE NOTE TO IT.

FORTE SIGN HAS
GRACEFUL CURVES

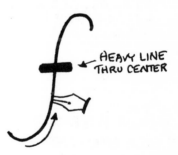

HEAVY LINE
THRU CENTER

HAIRPINS — FOR BRIEF RISE AND FALL OF
VOLUME. USE YOUR REGULAR PEN
OR YOUR SMALL PEN.

33

SLURS AND TIES

LONG SLURS ARE DRAWN BY HOLDING YOUR WRIST IN A LOCKED POSITION AND <u>SLOWLY</u> SLIDING YOUR HAND ACROSS THE PAGE.

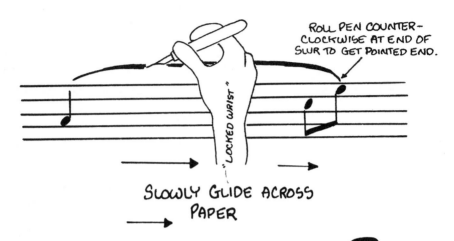

ROLL PEN COUNTER-CLOCKWISE AT END OF SLUR TO GET POINTED END.

"LOCKED WRIST"

SLOWLY GLIDE ACROSS PAPER

TIES ARE DRAWN THE SAME AS SLURS. TIES ALWAYS CONNECT THE NOTEHEADS, NEVER THE STEMS.

RIGHT:

WRONG:

SLUR PLACEMENT IS PRETTY FLEXIBLE. GENERALLY, THE SLUR GOES NEXT TO THE NOTEHEADS IN THE OPPOSITE DIRECTION OF THE STEMS.

LONG SLURS WILL GENERALLY GO ON TOP OF THE STAFF, REGARDLESS OF THE STEM DIRECTION.

ACCENTS

ALL ACCENTS ARE DRAWN FREEHAND

AS A GENERAL RULE PLACE ALL ACCENTS ON TOP OF THE NOTE AND ABOVE THE STAFF, REGARDLESS OF THE STEM DIRECTION. THIS CONSISTANCY MAKES IT EASIER FOR READING.

35

REPEATS

SINGLE MEASURE REPEAT

HEAVY SLASH DRAWN AT A 45° ANGLE BE-TWEEN THE SECOND AND FOURTH LINES WITH DOTS ON BOTH SIDES OF IT IN THE SECOND AND THIRD SPACES.

GENERALLY THERE ARE ONLY FOUR REPEATED BARS ON A LINE.

IF THERE ARE MORE THAN FOUR REPEATED BARS ON A LINE, INDICATE HOW MANY TIMES THE BAR IS REPEATED ABOVE THE FOURTH BAR AND IN THE LAST BAR ON THE LINE.

NUMBERS IN PARENTHESES

TWO MEASURE REPEAT

SIMILAR TO THE ONE MEA-SURE REPEAT, BUT WITH TWO HEAVY SLASHES INSTEAD OF ONE. IT'S BISECTED BY THE BAR LINE.

A SMALL '2', IN PARENTHESES, MAY BE DRAWN OVER THE REPEAT SIGN FOR CLARIFICATION.

NOTE: NEVER START A LINE WITH A REPEAT SIGN.

FOR MANY REPEATED MEASURES:

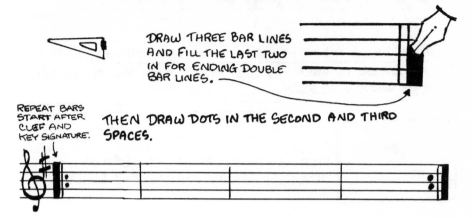

DRAW THREE BAR LINES AND FILL THE LAST TWO IN FOR ENDING DOUBLE BAR LINES.

THEN DRAW DOTS IN THE SECOND AND THIRD SPACES.

REPEAT BARS START AFTER CLEF AND KEY SIGNATURE.

BACK TO BACK REPEATS HAVE TWO HEAVY BARS.

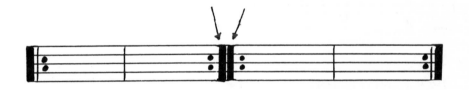

FIRST AND SECOND ENDINGS

USE YOUR SMALL PEN. LEAVE A BREAK IN THE LINE FOR THE NUMBER. PLACE A PERIOD AFTER THE NUMBER.

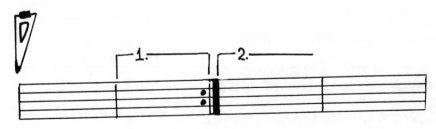

RHYTHM MARKS

<u>QUARTER NOTE RHYTHM MARK WITH NO STEM</u> - IS USED WHEN PLAYER IS FREE TO IMPROVISE ANY RHYTHM PATTERN HE WISHES TO PLAY.

HEAVY SLASH DRAWN AT 45° ANGLE BETWEEN SECOND AND FOURTH LINES.

QUARTER NOTE RHYTHM MARK "WITH STEM" AND EIGHTH NOTE RHYTHM MARKS ARE USED TO INDICATE SPECIFIC RHYTHM PATTERNS TO BE PLAYED.

<u>WHOLE NOTE RHYTHM MARK</u>

SHAPED LIKE A PARALLELOGRAM. USE YOUR SMALL PEN.

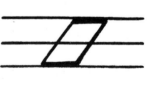

<u>HALF NOTE RHYTHM MARK</u>

SAME AS THE WHOLE NOTE RHYTHM MARK WITH THE STEM DRAWN OFF THE BOTTOM, LEFT CORNER OF THE PARALLELOGRAM.

SEGNO, CODA, FINE

SEGNO

PLACE ABOVE STAFF
AFTER BAR LINE.
(USE SMALL PEN)

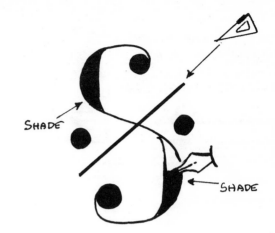

SHADE

SHADE

CODA

PLACE ABOVE STAFF
ALIGNED WITH BAR LINE.
(USE SMALL PEN)

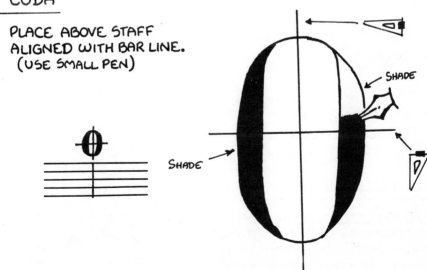

SHADE

SHADE

SHADE

PLACE ABOVE STAFF
(USE SMALL PEN)

UPPER CASE
LETTERS

HANDWRITTEN

D.S. al ⊕

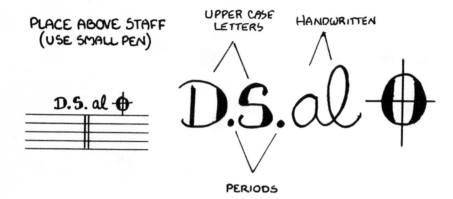

PERIODS

SIMILARLY:

D.C. al ⊕

PLACE BELOW STAFF
AFTER DOUBLE BAR LINE.
(USE SMALL PEN)

fine

fine

OCTAVE SIGNS

8va MEANS TO PLAY AN OCTAVE HIGHER THAN WHAT IS WRITTEN. USE YOUR SMALL PEN.

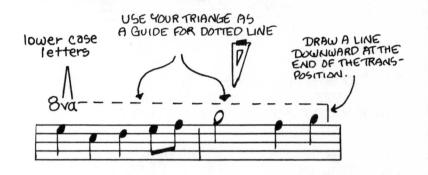

USE YOUR TRIANGE AS A GUIDE FOR DOTTED LINE

lower case letters

DRAW A LINE DOWNWARD AT THE END OF THE TRANSPOSITION.

8va bassa MEANS TO PLAY AN OCTAVE LOWER WHAT IS WRITTEN. USE YOUR SMALL PEN.

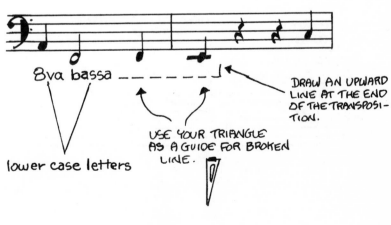

DRAW AN UPWARD LINE AT THE END OF THE TRANSPOSITION.

lower case letters

USE YOUR TRIANGLE AS A GUIDE FOR BROKEN LINE.

FERMATAS

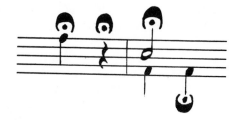

THE FERMATA IS GENERALLY PLACED OVER THE NOTE OR REST, UNLESS THERE'S TWO PARTS WRITTEN ON ONE STAFF OR AB-SOLUTELY NO PLACE TO WRITE IT THERE.

USE YOUR REGULAR PEN. DRAW HALF OF OF AN EGG WITH A DOT IN THE CENTER.

SHADE

TRILLS

USE YOUR SMALL PEN OR YOUR REGULAR PEN.

HANDWRITTEN LETTERS

WAVY LINE TO END OF TRILL

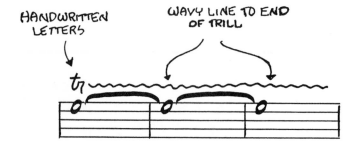

GRACE NOTES

DRAW A SMALL
SLUR FROM NOTE-
HEAD TO NOTEHEAD.

GRACE NOTES ARE ALWAYS
DRAWN STEMS UP. DRAW A
SLASH THRU THE FLAG AND
STEM.
(USE YOUR SMALL PEN)

GLISSANDOS

USE YOUR REGULAR PEN. SLOWLY DRAW A WAVY
LINE FROM NOTEHEAD TO NOTEHEAD.

TREMOLOS

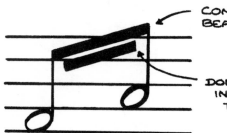

CONNECT OUTSIDE
BEAM TO STEMS.

DON'T CONNECT
INSIDE BEAM
TO STEMS.

DRAW SHORT, STUBBY
LINES FREEHAND WITH
YOUR REGULAR PEN.

BOWING MARKS

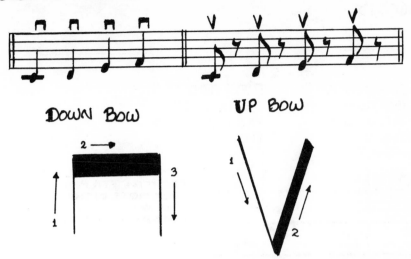

DOWN BOW

UP BOW

YOUR PEN HELD IN ITS NORMAL WRITING POSITION WILL PRODUCE THESE SHADINGS.

HARMONICS

ADD THE SMALL DIAMOND WITH YOUR SMALL PEN

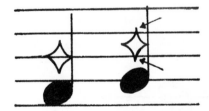

ON A SPACE NOTE HARMONIC, THE TOP AND BOTTOM OF THE DIAMOND EXTEND JUST SLIGHTLY INTO THE SPACES ON EITHER SIDE.

ADD THE SMALL CIRCLE WITH YOUR SMALL PEN

CHORDS

1.
DRAW THE
BOTTOM NOTE
FIRST WITH
THE STEM

2.
THEN ADD
THE REST OF
THE NOTES TO
THE CHORD

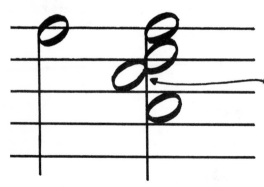

5TH — MAKE THE STEM EXTEND ABOUT A FIFTH PAST THE LAST NOTE IN THE CHORD. (THIS MAY VARY IN DIFFERENT CIRCUMSTANCES)

WHEN A 'SECOND' IS PRESENT IN A CHORD WITH AN 'UP STEM' OFFSET THE HIGHER OF THE TWO NOTES OFF TO THE RIGHT.

IN REVERSE:

THE LOWER NOTE OF THE SECOND GOES OFF TO THE LEFT WHEN THE CHORD HAS A 'DOWN STEM'.

ACCIDENTALS WITH CHORDS

TRY TO KEEP ACCIDENTALS FROM TOUCHING EACH OTHER.

IF THE DISTANCE BETWEEN THE TWO NOTES THAT REQUIRE ACCIDENTALS IS A SEVENTH OR MORE, THE TWO ACCIDENTALS SHOULD BE PERPENDICULARLY ALIGNED.

IF THE DISTANCE BETWEEN THE TWO NOTES THAT REQUIRE ACCIDENTALS IS LESS THAN A SEVENTH FROM TOP TO BOTTOM, ONE ACCIDENTAL GOES CLOSEST TO THE HIGHEST NOTE THAT HAS AN ACCIDENTAL AND THE OTHER IS OFFSET SLIGHTLY TO THE LEFT.

COMBINING THESE TWO RULES

WHEN SEVERAL ACCIDENTALS ARE WITH A CHORD TRY TO ALIGN TWO ACCIDENTALS IN CLOSE TO THE CHORD PERPENDICULARLY. THEN PLACE AN ACCIDENTAL CLOSEST TO THE HIGHEST OF THE REMAINING NOTES AND THE NEXT OFF TO THE LEFT.

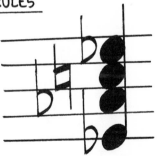

SIMILARLY:

ARPEGGIOS

USING YOUR REGULAR PEN. <u>SLOWLY</u> DRAW A WAVY LINE
PARALLEL TO THE CHORD.

A REGULAR ARPEGGIO PLAYED
FROM BOTTOM TO TOP.

A REVERSE ARPEGGIO PLAYED
FROM TOP TO BOTTOM.

BRINGING THE NOTES
TO REST ON PAPER SO
THE EYES CAN ENJOY
THEM AS MUCH AS THE
EARS IS THE FINAL COM-
PLIMENT TO A PIECE OF
MUSIC.

SPACING IN A MEASURE

A MEASURE SHOULD BE DIVIDED INTO AS MANY EQUAL PARTS AS THERE ARE BEATS. SPACING OF NOTES SHOULD BE DIRECTED BY THE TIME VALUES OF THE NOTES. A HALF NOTE TAKES UP HALF A MEASURE, A QUARTER NOTE TAKES UP A QUARTER OF A MEASURE, ETC.

C OMPLEX SITUATIONS OFTEN WON'T FOLLOW THIS SIMPLE DIVISION METHOD BUT, NONE THE LESS, MUST BE KEPT WELL BALANCED AND EVEN IN APPEARANCE FOR MAXIMUM LEGIBILITY. THE SPACE BETWEEN THE NOTES MUST BE CONSIDERED AND WEIGHED AS IN ANY KIND OF OVERALL DESIGN.

A LWAYS START WRITING AT THE VERY BEGINNING OF THE MEASURE

LIKE THIS:

NOT LIKE THIS:

CLEFS

WHETHER OR NOT A CLEF IS DRAWN AT THE BEGINNING OF EVERY LINE IS LARGELY A MATTER OF TASTE IN EACH DIFFERENT SITUATION.*

A KEY SIGNATURE SHOULD ALWAYS BE WRITTEN ON EVERY LINE.

KEY SIGNATURE CARRIED ON EVERY LINE WITH CLEF

OR CLEF MAY BE LEFT OFF

KEY AND TIME CHANGES

IF A KEY CHANGE COMES AT THE END OF A LINE, LEAVE A LITTLE SPACE AT THE END OF THE LINE AND DRAW THE CHANGE THERE AFTER A DOUBLE BAR. THEN START THE NEXT LINE WITH THE CHANGE DRAWN AGAIN.

A TIME CHANGE IS DRAWN SIMILARLY BUT NO DOUBLE BAR IS NECESSARY.

DOUBLE BAR BEFORE KEY CHANGE

DOUBLE BAR AGAIN AT THE BEGINNING OF THE LINE

NO DOUBLE IS NECESSARY FOR TIME CHANGES ALONE

*IN THE EXAMPLES HERE AND ON THE FOLLOWING PAGES YOU WILL SEE THE CLEF USED BOTH WAYS.

MEASURES ON A LINE

GENERALLY THERE ARE FOUR MEASURES ON A LINE. DON'T DIVIDE THE LINE OFF BY ANY MATHEMATICAL MEANS, BUT INSTEAD MAKE THE MEASURES SMALLER OR LARGE ENOUGH TO FILL THE NEEDS OF THE NOTES IN THE MEASURE. SPACING IS NOT A MATTER OF MECHANICS BUT RATHER OF FEELING AND TASTE.

SOME SITUATIONS WILL CALL FOR MORE OR LESS THAN FOUR MEASURES ON A LINE.

TITLES

ALThough many styles of lettering may be used for titling a piece of music the one you see on this page is the most common.

The letters are very much like regular block letters, but they have a more rounded quality to them, almost cartoon like in their character.

Use a "Speedball" B-1 or B-2 nib.

A secret to good lettering is in single strokes. Lift the pen after every stroke.

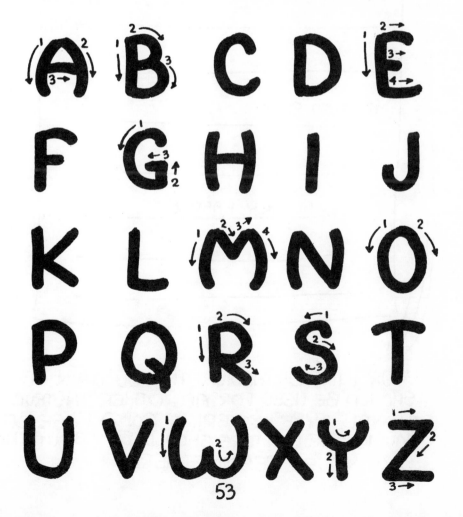

CENTER THE TITLE BETWEEN THE FIRST
TWO STAVE LINES. THE SIZE OF THE LETTERS IS
VARIABLE. ANYWHERE FROM ½" TO ¾."

WRITE INSTRUMENT NAME
IN UPPER LEFT CORNER.

WRITE COMPOSERS NAME
UNDER TITLE, TO THE RIGHT.

FLUTE
PATHETIQUE
L. BEETHOVEN

GRAVE

TO ALTO FLUTE

SLIGHTLY FASTER

YOUR FINE-OR MEDIUM-TIP FOUNTAIN PEN
SHOULD BE USED FOR ALL OTHER "INSTRUC-
TIONAL" TYPE LETTERING ON A PAGE OF
MUSIC. THE LETTERS SHOULD BE ABOUT THE
SIZE YOU'RE READING HERE.

54

BAR NUMBERS

Bar numbers and/or rehearsal letters are used for reference points when several people are reading a piece of music. Use your medium tip fountain pen.

FLUTE

FALLING IN

HERONOMOUS ANONYMOUS

©1977 GLEN ROSECRANS

CHORD SYMBOLS

KEEP CHORD SYMBOLS LARGE AND CLEAR. USE YOUR MEDIUM TIP FOUNTAIN PEN.

PIANO

LIMITATIONS

NELG SNARCESOR

SLOW CHA-CHA

CHORD PARTS

WHEN WRITING CHORD PARTS TAKE EXTRA CARE TO KEEP THE
NOTES IN ALIGNMENT. (NOTICE THE DIFFERENT LETTERING STYLE
USED FOR THE TITLE OF THIS PIECE.)

Prélude
Op. 28 No. 7

F. Chopin

Bibliography

BORNSTEIN, ROBERT. ~ RANGE & TRANSPOSITION GUIDE. WIM. LOS ANGELES, 1964.

DONATO, ANTHONY ~ PREPARING MUSIC MANUSCRIPT. NEW YORK: AMSCO, 1963.

DOUGLAS, RALPA ~ CALLIGRAPHIC LETTERING. WATSON-GUPTILL.

GEORGE, ROSS F. ~ SPEEDBALL ELEMENTARY ALPHABETS. PHILADELPHIA: HUNT 1940.

JOHNSON, HAROLD M. ~ HOW TO WRITE MUSIC MANUSCRIPT. NEW YORK: FISCHER, 1956.

McKAY, GEORGE F. ~ CREATIVE ORCHESTRATION. BOSTON: ALLYN & BACON INC., 1969.

READ, GARDNER ~ MUSIC NOTATION. BOSTON: CRESCENDO PUBLISHERS, 1969.

ROEMER, CLINTON ~ THE ART OF MUSIC COPYING. ROERICK MUSIC. SHERMAN OAKS 1973.

ROSS, TED ~ THE ART OF MUSIC ENGRAVING AND PROCESSING. S.F.: HANSEN, 1970.

ABOUT THE AUTHOR....

GLEN ROSECRANS HAS WORKED IN THE MOTION PICTURE INDUSTRY SINCE 1967 AS A COPYIST AND AUTOGRAPHER, LEARNING THE TRADE FROM HIS FATHER.

HE NOW RESIDES IN SANTA CRUZ, CALIF., WHERE HE'S ACTIVELY INVOLVED IN THE MUSIC SCENE AND IS TEACHING AT CABRILLO COLLEGE.